S0-BQT-276

For Elizabeth and Carrol
with best wishes,
Lisa

From My

Texan Log Cabin

Aus meiner
texanischen Blockhütte

LISA KAHN

EAKIN PRESS

Austin, Texas

When the name of the translator is not mentioned, the poems have been rendered into English by the author who gratefully acknowledges the assistance of Edna Brown.

Falls nicht anders vermerkt, wurden die Gedichte von der Autorin übersetzt. Für Hilfe bei dieser Arbeit sei Edna Braun herezlich gedankt.

The pen drawings are by Peter Kahn who studied Geology and German at Rice University, University of Tübingen, Princeton and Freie Universität Berlin. He has exhibited drawings and lithographs at the Jewish Community Center in Houston and at Princeton.

Die Federzeichnungen stammen von Peter Kahn. Nach Doppelstudium der Geologie und Germanistik an der Rice Universität studierte er in Tübingen, Princeton und an der Freien Universität Berlin. Ausstellungen von Zeichnungen und Lithographien in Houston und Princeton.

The following poems have been published in German only:

Homecoming and Farewell — in *Klingsor,* Suny at Buffalo, N.Y.
Eden — in *Klopfet an so wird euch nicht aufgetan,* Darmstadt, 1975
February Night in Texas — in *Humanities in the South,* Fall 1980
Hoarfrost — in *Feuersteine,* Zürich, 1978
Wieder Texas — in *Denver im Frühling,* Darmstadt, 1980
This is a love Story — in *David am Komputer,* Providence, R.I., 1982
Old Cemetery in Texas — in *Nachrichten aus den Staaten,* 1983
I thank the publishers and editors for permission to reprint.

Copyright © 1984
By Lisa Kahn

Published in the United States of America
By Eakin Press, P.O. Box 23066, Austin, Texas 78735

ALL RIGHTS RESERVED

ii

Für

Anna, Dona, Edna, Elizabeth,
Inge, Ingrid, Mary,
Peter and Thecla

CONTENTS

INHALTSFOLGE

v

Foreword

I have on numerous occasions lamented the fact that the poetry of our foremost modern German Texan poet has not been accessible to the majority of German Texans, and has been almost completely inaccessible to other Texans. To be sure, the outstanding journal providing the American audience access to contemporary German literature, *Dimension,* has published a sample of her work, as have other American journals. Nevertheless, many Texans are unaware of what a treasure they have in Texas. Even the many Texans who know Lisa Kahn from her efforts in education and in community work in Houston and in Round Top may not all realize the diversity and remarkable quality of her poetry. None of her previous collections of poetry has had facing translations, and none has been restricted to her 'Texas' poems. The decision to make this restriction, though it deprives her readers of the broad range of her themes, has resulted in a volume that speaks to us in Texas directly and thus can only be applauded.

Dr. Hubert Heinen
Associate Professor of German
The University of Texas at Austin

Lisa Kahn beweist mit jedem Gedicht, wie lieb ihr ihre Muttersprache ist.
Sie ist eine Kuenstlerin der Lyrik, die ihre zweite Heimat, Texas, mit einem reichen dichterischen Ton malt.
Ihre texanischen Gedichte stellen diesen vielseitigen Staat mit einem beeindruckenden Sprachreichtum vor.
Ob sie ueber die Golfkueste, Round top, den Big Bend oder ueber Lubbock dichtet, man fuehlt sich durch Lisa Kahn's Dichtung in seiner eigenen Betrachtung bestaetigt.

Ingrid Kuehne Kokinda
Consultant, German-Texan
Heritage Society

Introduction

Neither in Berlin nor in Leipzig where I spent my formative years, neither in Heidelberg nor in Seattle where I studied and then started my own family, was there ever enough time to grow roots. Not until I came to Round Top, Texas, to live on my little "place" (as the German-Texans put it so aptly), did I find roots. There in my self-chosen solitude, I can examine myself and my life. There I gain the distance to do so. There my experience is shattered into a multitude of small mosaic pieces which are then assembled anew in language.

Of course, memory is not identical with memory. New stimuli, new elements, new associations are added to each experience, each memory, so that in the process of changing, often completely new vistas emerge. This may be a slow step-by-step process or a volcanic-like eruption. Thus the original events are transformed into novel imagery and figurations.

And when poetry or prose are written in the first person, that does not mean that the lyrical "I" is identical with the "I" of the author.

Well, it is high time now that the poems should speak for themselves.

Einführung

Weder in Berlin noch in Leipzig, wo ich meine formativen Jahre verlebte, weder in Heidelberg noch in Seattle, wo ich studierte und dann die eigene Familie gründete, blieb genügend Zeit, um Wurzeln zu schlagen. Erst in Roun dTop, auf dem kleinen "Platz," wie die Texaner in dieser deutschsprachigen Gegend so nett sagen, habe ich endlich Wurzeln gefunden. Dort, in meiner selbstgewählten Einsamkeit, entsteht dann die Auseinandersetzung mit mir selbst und mit meinem Leben. Dort wird der Abstand gewonnen. Dort wird Erfahrung in viele kleine Mosaiksteine zersplittert und in Sprache neu zusammengesetzt.

Dabei ist selbstverständlich Erinnerung nicht gleich Erinnerung. Zu jeder Erfahrung, jedere Erinnerung kommen neue Reize, neue Elemente, neue Assoziationen, sodass umgewandelte, oft ganz neue Erinnerungsbilder entstehen. Das mag ein langsamer stufenweiser Prozess sein oder ein vulkanartiger Ausbruch. So weerden ursprüngliche Ereignisse in neue Erlebnisbilder umgeformt.

Und wenn Gedichte oder Prosa in der Ich-Form geschrieben sind, so heisst das nicht, dass das lyrische Ich etwa mit dem Ich des Autors identisch ist.

Aber nun wird es höchste Zeit, die Gedichte selbst sprechen zui lassen.

OLD HOUSE

Crooked from sighs
the worn stairs but the
painted roof, still representing the
same view of the oaken giants though
here a branch is split and
there a bough fallen and over
there the blackness of a green
wound from lightning brings pain
a thousand new leaves all around
coincidence the name of the
master-sorcerer's miracles
you ask: why do you grow here
instead of a thousand yards beyond?
Why am I myself and not my
brother? Why is this berry red
and that one blue? Why did you cross
this threshold never to return home?

ALTES HAUS

die ausgetretenen Stiegen
seufzergekrümmt aber vom Spitzdach
noch immer der gleiche der Blick
auf die Eichenriesen obschon
hier ein Ast geborsten
da einer abgefallen dort eine
schwarze Blitzwunde noch frisch
schmerzend
tausend neue Blätter rings
Zufall heisst der Wunder Zaubermeister
Fragst du: warum stehst du hier und
nicht tausend Meter weiter?
Warum bin ich ich anstatt mein
Bruder? Warum ist die Beere rot
und jene blau? Warum gingst du über
diese Schwelle niemals heimzukehren?

1

MEADOW

On the softly bobbing ocean of silvery green
the colorful dots luminous and pastel
no little victory garden diligently
watered no Eden for here birds eat
gnats the child catches butterflies
nevertheless an approximation of
loveliness

WIESE

Auf leise wogendem Meer aus Silbergrün
die bunten Tupfen leuchtend und zart
kein Schrebergarten artig bewässert
kein Eden denn hier frißt der Vogel
die Mücke fängt das Kind den Falter
immerhin eine Annäherung an das
Liebliche

I roused
the false wind
now I'm alone
on my way to heaven-knows-where

the shadow whispers:
when the sun sets
you'll lose me

I didn't realize
how right he was
I should have known!
could I have?

Den falschen Wind
habe ich aufgeweckt
jetzt bin ich allein
unterwegs nach werweisswohin

flüstert der Schatten: wenn
die Sonne sinkt wirst du
mich verlieren

wie recht er hatte
ich wusste es nicht
hätt es doch wissen sollen!
konnte ich?

A DAY

A day so it seemed
for aiming low for
practicing to be unassuming
for attempting the practice
of holding back and for
attempts at such attempts

yet sweeping away our
powerlessness it turned
into a wild untamed day
a day of impropriety
a day of death

EIN TAG

Ein Tag so schien es um
sich zu bescheiden
das Sichbescheiden einzuüben
für Versuche des Einübens
von Sichbescheiden und
Versuche von Versuchen

aber unsere Machtlosigkeit
hinwegfegend wurde es ein
wilder ein ungezähmter
ein ungebührlicher Tag
ein Todestag

EVENINGS

Light flows back
into itself now for a
small span of time
things seem to lack
their purpose destination
floating freely through
space reflected only
through us reminding
you of something of
which you have no memory

AM ABEND

Das Licht fliesst nun in
sich selbst zurück für
eine kleine Spanne Zeit
Scheinen die Dinge ihrer
Bestimmung entzogen
schweben frei im Raum
spiegeln sich nur durch
uns erinnern dich an etwas
woran du keine Erinnerung hast

Moon light
the deposit of calcium in
coronary capillaries
non-stop
heartaches

the chisel of dreams
lays bare the shape
hidden in the stone
who cares about pain?
morning arrives

Mondenes Licht
die Kalkablagerung in
den Kranzgefässen
pausenlos
Herzsorgen

der Meissel des Traums
schält die Gestalt
aus dem Stein wer
achtet der Schmerzen?
Es wird Morgan

LUNA

Luna
Moon
my ally
softly do I want to beckon
you now that I have
recognized you as a woman

it is summer
your full face
no longer ghastly
announcing evil
is soft
mother moon

LUNA

Luna
Mondin
Verbündete
zärtlich will ich dir
winken nun da ich dich als
Frau erkannt

es ist Sommer
dein volles Gesicht
nicht länger schrecklich
Unheil verkündend
es ist weich
Mutter Mond

FULL MOON OVER HOUSTON

Gleaming glittering heat over an
ocean of houses and prairies
and already you rise at the high blue horizon
fully born
golden yellow
a glutton's fleshy face
an imitation of the Threepenny opera moon
a lampion
for garden parties
large and close to the touch
toy ball for children of giants
and as useless
hello you pug-face up there
soon our astronauts will explore
whether you turn red with rage
you superannuated compass you
needless meteorologist
old-fashioned symbol of the Romantics
ridiculous comforter of melancholy poets
you can't even compete with neon moons
though you happen to be big today
you jerk
made of salmon colored crape paper
you operetta moon from Samoa
you ocre-shaded dumpling!
we fools mock you
you plump-cheeked
round messsenger made
of red gold

VOLLMOND ÜBER HOUSTON

Hellflimmernde Hitze über Häusermeer
und Steppe
und schon kommst du am hohen blauen Horizont herauf
voll geboren
goldgelb
ein feistes Völlergesicht
eine Dreigroschenopernimitation
ein Lampion
bei einer Gartenparty
gross und zum Greifen nah
Spielball für Riesenkinder
und so nutzlos
hallo du Mops da oben
bald erforschen unsere Astronauten
ob du auch rot wirst vor Zorn
ausgedienter Kompass du
nutzloser Wetterprophet
Überholtes Symbol der Romantiker
lächerlicher Trostspender für melancholische Odenschreiber!
Kannst nicht mal mit Neonmonden konkurrieren
obschon du heute so gross geraten
du Trottel
aus lachsfarbenem Krepp
du Operettenmond aus Samoa
du ockerfarbener Kloss!
Wir Toren mockieren uns über dich
du vollbackiger
runder Raumbote
aus rotem Gold

AGAIN: TO THE MOON

Reddish golden
a slight half
of a wedding band
you blink from the
darkness of rainclouds
a tiny swing
between Sadducees
and Pharisees
Elitists and
Populists
Catholics
Communists
Environmentalists
wish and reality
between me and
me

WIEDER: AN DEN MOND

Rotgolden
ein schmaler
halber Ehering
blinkst du aus
Regenwolkendun-
kel
eine klitzekleine
Schiffschaukel
zwischen Saduzäern
und Pharisäern
Elitären und
Populisten
Schwarzen Grünen
Roten
Wunsch und
Wirklichkeit
zwischen mir und
mir

11

WOLF IN ROUND TOP

The wolf
whom I traced
his nocturnal howl
still in my ear at morning
disappeared into the
black cedar grove

their shade blocks my
view the barbed wire
keeps me but not the thief
from entering the forest
shall I climb the fence crawl
underneath pull the branches
apart stalk him on the
paths of silence?

but should I find him
who will show me the
passage back?

WOLF IN ROUND TOP

Der Wolf
dem ich auf der Spur
sein nächtlich Heulen
noch früh im Ohr
verschwand unter den
schwarzen Zedern

ihre Schatten verstellen
den Blick der Stachel-
drahtzaun wehrt mir
nicht dem Räuber den
Waldwechsel soll ich
hinüberklettern
hindurchschlupfen
die Zweige auseinander-
biegen ihm auf den
Pfaden des Schweigens
nachschleichen?

aber falls ich ihn finde
wer wird mir den Weg
zurückweisen?

No peace over the tree-tops
you sense fire and the reek of blood
war screams in the forest
rages over acres of ruins
never will you find rest

Über keinem Wipfel ist Ruh
Brand und Blutdunst spürest du
Krieg heult im Walde
tobt auf Trümmerhalde
nie ruhest du

Who will bring back your image
to me your shape?

not my oak trees they
are rooted firmly

not my lizards
without memory

my snakes with their
tiny clever little heads

but they know better

Wer holt mir dein Bild
zurück deine Gestalt?

meine Eichen nicht die
sind festgewurzelt

meine Echsen nicht die
gedächtnislosen

meine Schlangen mit
zierlichen klugen Köpfchen

aber die wissens besser

HOMECOMING AND FAREWELL

Open heart-folio long laid out before him his landscape
in daydreams nightdreams nightmares
           (she drew him to the light)

openheart-folio
his house self-carpentered
upon whose rafters he dripped tears and sweat

a thousand times in the alien distance he
bestrode his fields
checked his fences
stepped on his threshold
and heard the radiant welcome of his mother
heart-agitated
and now his wishes fulfilled

surrounded by green
bedded in gold
and green again

the white bench
the red berries shine
the warm breath of his brown-and-white spotted herd steams
their coats glisten
and the childhood gladness
is near as yesterday
his hope-heart in both hands
he knocks
and all grids grates gates doors
spring open
from all nooks crannies and recesses
greetings resound
echo-repeated

in his veins arteries even in the coronary capillaries throbs joy
throbs fear: HOW to take leave again
from his roots?
What process of self-disection is required here?
How many times can he survive this torture
he whose heart is not
where he must be
and who is not allowed to stay
where poppy and lillies bloom

translated by Minetta Altgelt Goyne

HEIMKEHR UND ABSCHIED

Herzaufgeblättert lange vor ihm gelegen
seine Landschaft
in Tagträumen, Nachtträumen, Albträumen
(da zog sie ihn ins Licht)
herzaufgeblättert
sein Haus selbstgezimmert
dessen Balken er tränen– und schweissbetropft

tausendmal in der fremden Ferne
seine Felder beschritten
sein Zäune geprüft
seine Schwelle betreten
der Mutter helles Willkommen gehört
herzaufgewühlt
und nun die Wünsche erfüllt

von Grün umfangen
in Gold gebettet
und wieder Grün

die weisse Bank
die roten Beeren leuchten
der warme Maulhauch seiner braun– und weissgefleckten Herde

dampft
die Felle glänzen
und der Kindheit Frohsein
ist so nah wie gestern

sein Hoffnungsherz in beiden Händen
klopft er an
und alle Gitter Gatter Tore Türen
springen auf
aus allen Winkeln Ecken und Verstecken
schallt Grüssen
echowiederholt

in seinen Venen Adern bis in alle Kranzgefässe
pocht Glück
pocht Angst: WIE von seinen Wurzeln
Wieder Abschied nehmen?
Welcher Selbstzerstückelungsprozess wird hier verlangt?
Wieviele Male kann diese Folter überstehn
des Herz nicht ist
wo er sein muss
der nicht darf sein
wo Mohn und Lilie blühn

LISTENING

put your ear
to the meadow's lap
to better hear grass
and hemp growing the
chattering of bugs the
laughter of fish
the gathering of waters
deep down and the song of
your own veins

HORCHEN

Dein Ohr halte
an den Wiesenschoss
besser das Wachsen von
Gras und Hanf zu hören
das Geschwätz der Käfer
das Lachen der Fische
das Sammeln der Wasser tief
drunten und den Sang deiner
eigenen Adern

UNEXPECTED

I spoke: Open Sesame!
and icy flakes fell from
the fairy's featherbed
the billy club jumped
out of its holster maggots
crawled out of Pandora's box

UNERWARTET

Ich sprach: Sesamöffnedich!
und es purzelten eisige
Flocken aus Frau Holles
Plumeau der Knüppel hüpfte
aus dem Sack Würmer krochen
aus Pankdoras Büchse

VERBENA

Verbena Verbena (wer bin ich? wer bin ich?)
and bluebonnets bloom
towards my heart now
that poems and stories
have crept into ears
and laid down to sleep
on my lips in the dusk

Verbena and Indian paintbrush
puerile guardians of your
grave when under the new moon
green turns black
they sing in the darkness
fold their petals to protect
your heart

they drop their dreams
onto you wake you up your
hands start sprouting
through hard soil and crumbs
and in the greening of spring
your bed is strewn
with Verbena Verbena (wer bin ich? wer bin ich?)

                    Translated by Minetta Altgeld Goyne

VERBENA

Verbena Verbena (wer bin ich? wer bin ich?)
und blaue Hütchen blüht
herzwärts nun
da Gedichte Geschichten
sich im Dämmern
ins Ohr geschlichen
auf Lippen gelegt

Verbena and indianische Pinselblume
Kinderwächter auf deinem
Grab wenn unterm neuen Mond
sich das Grün schwarz verfärbt
singen im Dunkel
falten die Blättchen
herzschützend

tropfen ihre Träume auf
dich die wecken dich auf
deine Hände spriessen
durch Scholle und Krume
und im Frühlingsgrün
ist dein Bett besät
mit Verbenea Verbenea (wer bin ich? wer bin ich?)

NEIGHBOR

Back bent
the heavy man
still carved of wood?
he stands on the threshold
silent as is his custom

his gaze still light and keen
rising from beds of deep crow's feet
roams along the horizon
waiting for signals of rain
rests proud or fearful
on pasture and cattle

when the red ball of a sun
drops into the blackness
of cedars he plops on the sofa
turns on the TV:

hey Mom that dinner was really delicious
she can hardly trust her ears
could there be something wrong with him?
then she smiles softly with her
eyes forgets that tomorrow it will
be that day again their only child
died

NACHBAR

fr Wilbert M.

Krummen Rückens
der schwere Mann
ist er aus Holz geschnitzt?
steht auf der Schwelle
schweigt wie gewohnt

sein Blick noch hellscharf
kommt aus tiefen
Krähenfussbetten
schweift immer noch suchend
horizontentlang
wartet auf Regenzeichen
ruht stolz oder ängstlich
auf Weide und Vieh

fällt die rote Sonnenkugel
ins Zedernschwarz
plumpst er aufs Sofa
schaltet den Fernseher an:

Na Muttern heut hats aber geschmeckt
die traut ihren Ohren nicht
ob was los ist mit ihm?
dann lächelt sie leis mit den
Augen vergisst dass morgen
des einzigen Kindes Todestag

CHANGE

Bench facing the sunset
once you stood a beaming bride
in the green clover happy as in
folksongs and children's rhymes

after all these summers bursting
with heat tropical downpours
the shivering contractions in Januaries
fallen apart replaced by a new
one solid weatherproofed with
Penta strong golden brown
unburdened by memories let us
turn it 180 degrees around
so it will face east!

WECHSEL

Sonnenuntergangsbank
einst strahlende Braut
weiss im grünen Klee
glücklich wie in Volks–
und Kinderliedern

nach all den hitzeprallen
Sommern strömenden Tropengüssen
dem fröstelnden Zusammenziehn
in Januaren zerfallen durch
eine neue ersetzt stabil
wetterschutzlackiert fest
goldbraun erinnerungsfrei
drehen wir sie doch um 180 Grad
dass sie nach Osten schaue!

A dead mouth sings
under an old tree
and the stones join
in the little ones
the wild flowers
the rabbits
the heat chants
the sun
but the grave
it keeps silent

A dead mouth sings
under an old tree
und die Steine stimmen
ein die kleinen
die Wiesenblumen
die Hasen
die Hitze singt
die Sonne
aber das Grab
das schweigt

27

SKY ABOVE TEXAS

Endless blue dome
or a circus tent for God
and the Ark Noah's animals
a gigantic plate cover for cheese
stretching over the prairie
over the tiny skyscrapers
the perpetually pumping
Liliputian refinery towers
over the toy chateaux of the millionaires
and the doll houses of the millions
everyone hurrying
like busy ants
back and forth
here and there
in colorful little gas guzzlers
from one end of the vault
to the other
and the other
and the other
sometimes the brilliant cupola
will permit the piling up of clouds
as a festive
or threatening scenery
then we insects gaze worried
or longingly towards the
massive cloud formations
the bizarre humps of gray water camels
and sometimes
when the huge bell is filled to bursting
with glass-clear heat
when the air gleams so white that
the blinded eye cries out loud with pain
then we laugh our cheers
our hottest laughter right into
the inverted gigantic blue pot

HIMMEL ÜBER TEXAS

Unendlicher blauer Dom
oder ein Zirkuszelt für Gott
und Noah und die Archentiere
eine Käseglocke für Riesen
über eine Steppe gestülpt
über die winzigen Wolkenkratzer
über die pausenlos pumpenden
Liliput-Petroleumtürme
über die Spielzeugchateaux der Millionäre
über die Puppenhäuschen der Millionen
alles flitzt
wie emige Ameisen
hin und her
her und hin
in farbenprächtigen Strassenkreuzerlein
von einem Ende
des endlosen Gewölbes
zum nächsten
und nächsten
und nächsten
manchmal duldet die blanke Kuppel
das Auftürmen von Wolkengebirgen
als festliche Szenerie
oder drohende
dann blicken wir Insekten besorgt
oder sehnsüchtig
auf die wuchtigen Wolkenmassen
die bizarren Höcker der grauen Wasserkamele
und zuweilen
wenn die gigantische Glocke
zum Bersten mit glasklarer Hitze gefüllt ist
wenn die Luft so weiss leuchtet
dass das geblendete Auge laut schmerzt
dann lachen wir unser hellstes
unser heissestes Lachen
in den umgestülpten Riesenblautopf

K 1

für Edna

In the shortlived dusk
stripes of sombre evening glow
settle quickly
on the horizon
anxiety
superstition rise
layers out of our own Cambrium

but the sun-tortured soil takes
a breath refreshed by the cool air
brought on tiptoes by the wind

K 1

Schnell lagern sich in der kurzlebigen
Dämmerung die Streifen düstern Abendrots
am Horizont
es stehen auf:
Angst
Aberglaube
Schichten aus unserm eigenen Cambrium

nur der sonnengequälte Boden atmet auf
labt sich an Kühle die der Wind auf
Zehenspitzen bringt

K 2

Baked by the blaze the earth dreams
of her lover he is perfidious
all the more passionately the wind
courts her whom she dislikes

rejected by her he takes revenge:
dishevels her harvest robe
tortures her skin for weeks on end
until the wide cracks have hard
scabs

one day he for whom she longs
will caress and heal her again
she is waiting in silence

K 2

Glutgedörrt träumt die Erde
vom Liebsten der ist treulos
umso heftiger wirbt den sie
nicht mag der Wind

abgeschüttelt rächt er sich:
zerfledert das Erntekleid
foltert die Haut wochenlang
bis die breiten Risse hart
verkrustet

eines Tages wird der Ersehnte
sie wieder liebkosen heilen
stumm wartet sie

EDEN

Are there roses
in the garden of Eden?
blackbirds?

The gate is closed
I can only sense
that behind it flowers are in bloom

Sometimes
a leaf drifts
a gentle sound of the flute

to me
thank you
wind

EDEN

Gibt es Rose,
Im Garten Eden?
Amseln?

Die Pforte ist zu
Ahnen nur kann ich
Daß drinnen Blumen blühn

Zuweilen weht
Ein Blatt heraus
Ein leiser Flötenklang

Zu mir
Danke
Wind

JANUARY IN ROUND TOP

Over night spring has placed
a white narcissus
on my grave
spring-green
white-washed
it stands a stranger in the weed afflicted
brown grass of an
unkempt workdawy
says: you want to try it
once more? Knows that
I was ready to throw in
the towel —
All right let's try it
once more

JANUAR IN ROUND TOP

Über Nacht hat der Frühling
mir eine weisse Narzisse
aufs Grab gesetzt
so frühlingsgrün
so weiss gewaschen
steht fremd im unkrautbedrängten
braunen Gras im
ungekämmten Alltag
sagt: willst dus nochmal
versuchen? Weiss
dass ich schon bereit die
Flinte ins Korn —
Ja versuchen wirs
einmal noch

CHANGING LANDSCAPE

Just a few months
gone from
this landscape in
whose latitudes the humid
heat quickens the pace
of growth
maturity
decomposition

yesterday's sapling
today's tree
today's love
tomorrow's death
               meanwhile the heaven opens in thousand
               tiny slits to let starlight through or
               draws rain-curtains before the burning blue

underneath rotting trunks
the bleached armor-hump-shields
of turtles which did not escape
on the porch transparent skin
long left behind by copperheads

               I left my Self here or at least a part
               of me are you able to do the same?

brown wintergrass now
turning a faint green and my retina
full of anticipation of the colorful
dotted print of wild flowers

the ponds shrunken
due to lack of rain

strange how another person whom one
believes to know so well can remain hidden
stranger still how he possesses such a power

just a few months
gone from this
landscape in
which the humid heat
hastens changes
consistently blooming
consistently withering
a sharp dull pain

VERÄNDERUNGEN IN DER LANDSCHAFT

Nur ein paar Monate
fortgewesen von
diesem Landstrich in
dessen Breite die feuchte
Hitze alles beschleunigt:
Wachsen
Reifen
Verfall

was gestern Sprössling
ist heute Baum
was heute Liebe
morgen Tod

> dawischen das Öffnen des Himmels in
> tausend kleine Schlitze für Sternenlicht
> oder ein Zuziehen von Regengardinen vor
> dem brennenden Blau

unter morschen Stämmen
ausgebleichter Panzerbuckelschild
nicht entkommener Kröte
auf der Veranda die transparente
Haut der die kupferköpfige Schlange
längst entschlüpft

> ich lass mich zurück oder doch einen Teil
> von mir kannst du das auch?

braunes Wintergras nun wieder
grün angehaucht und auf der Netzhaut
schon geahnt das bunte Tupfenbild
der wilden Blumen

36

die Teiche wegen Regenmangel
eingeschrumpft

> seltsam wie ein andrer Mensch den man so
> gut zu kennen glaubt verborgen bleibt
> seltsamer noch wie er solche Macht besitzt

nur ein paar Monate
fortgewesen von
diesem Landstrich in
dem die feuchte
Hitze schnelle
Veränderungen fördert
beständig blüht
beständig welkt
ein scharfer dumpfer Schmerz

MME TORTOISE

for Edna

Went strolling alone in the virgin forest
fresh dewberries were on my mind
there crawled Mrs. Turtle from under a
bush nodded friendly I said
Hi! do you mind a trip to the city so I
can show you to my kids? You are a gorgeous
specimen of your species and imagine
the chance to serve as a demonstration
model that's something not offered to just
any turtle
quickly I grabbed her buried her under
berries in my shopping basket then
back to the cottage filled the berries
into jars and noticed that she had hidden
timidly in her shell having left tiny
granules of dirt behind — gee that in her
fright her colon would show such a human
reaction! Or is our digestive system still
on the turtle level? So touched I put the
shell-sheltered lady back into the basket
carried her to the familiar shrub: Farewell
beware of fox and falcon! So long
until next weekend very gracefully she
pushes the little head out of her rigid house
the clever miniature eyes look round about
whether the giant enemy has gone — do I
hear her sigh of relief? Death or what she
took for it passed by this time

MADAME SCHILDKRÖTE

Ich ging im Urwald so für mich hin
die wilden Brombeern das war mein Sinn
da kroch Frau Schildkröte aus dem Gebüsch
freundlich kopfnickend so sag ich
Grüss Gott haben Sie etwas gegen eine
kleine Reise in die Stadt damit ich Sie
meinen Kindern zeigen kann? Sie sind ein
prächtiges Exemplar Ihrer Gattung und
bedenken Sie nur die Chance als Instruktions-
modell zu dienen das wird nicht jeder
Schildkröte geboten
stracks hob ich sie auf begrub sie
unter Beeren in meinem Henkelkorb
zurück zur Hütte das Obst in Gläser umgefüllt
sah wie sie sich scheu versteckt in ihrer
Schale und kleine Körnchen Dreck im Korb
gelassen — ach dass in Ängsten der Verdauungs-
apparat so menschlich reagiert! Oder steht
unser Digestivsystem noch auf der Schild-
krötstufe? Gerührt packt ich die horn-
geschützte Dame wieder in den Korb trug
sie zum alten Strauch: Leb wohl und
hüte dich vor Fuchs und Falke! Tschüs bis
zum nächsten Wochenend sehr zierlich schiebt
das Köpfchen sich aus steifer Hülle die klugen
Äuglein lugen um und um ob sich der Riesenfeind
verzogen — hör ich den Seufzer der Erleichterung?
Tod oder was ihr so erschien ging diesmal
noch vorüber

FEBRUARY NIGHT IN TEXAS

The fist of frost
behind your glitter
Orion
relaxed now
but the wolves' howling
still clearly heard

Spanish moss beards of
gnarled oaks hang tranquil
curtains to our secrets
behind which crouches
pain
flares up
jumps glaringly into
night's blackness

climbs a pale morning
sneakily along
we find ashes on
our threshold
but no smelted
ore.

FEBRUARNACHT IN TEXAS

Keine Frostfaust mehr
hinter deinem Glitzern
Orion

aber noch deutlich hörbar
das Heulen
der Wölfe

Moosbärte der alten Eichen
hängen still
Vorhänge unserer Heimlichkeit

hinter der Schmerz hockt
lodert
grell in die Schwarznacht springt

Schleicht ein bleicher Morgen hervor
finden wir Asche auf der Schwelle
darin kein geläutert Erz

MEADOW IN SUMMER

This is the year of the butterflies!

When ever did so many of them assail you?
excited fluttering noiselessly they cause
tender collisions with your arms and legs
throat and forehead: peacock butterflies
in mourning petites lemoncolored ones
others reddish-brown golden
butter-yellow canarycolored with
tiny black dots white ones so small
as if they were baby moths and all
of them eagerly heading for your
tanned limbs which — who knows —
they may consider to be blossom goals
or are you just an obstacle to their
June games a superfluous being who is
in the way of animals and plants?

SOMMERWIESE

Dies ist das Jahr der Schmetterlinge!

Wann hätten je so viele dich bestürmt?
aufgeregt flatternd geräuschlos
prallen sie zärtlich gegen Arme
Beine Hals und Stirn: Pfauenaugen
der Trauer und zierliche zitronen-
gelbe rotbraune goldne buttergelbe
kanarienfarbne mit winzigschwarzen
Punkten weisse so klein als seien sie
Mottenkinder und alle eifrig deine
sonnverbrannten Glieder ansteuernd
die sie vielleicht für Blütenziele
halten oder bist du nur Hindernis ihren
Junispielen ein überflüssiger Mensch
der Tier und Pflanze stört?

42

FAYETTE COUNTY, TEXAS, IN SUMMER

This land hard as a rock
thirsty under the wiry grass
the wild thorns
its dried out pond-eyes
stare into the blue yonder
today tomorrow for weeks on end
have given up their hope for rain
as we have ours for tears

this land has seemingly resigned
itself with waiting with drought
a resignation we still defy
with our work

KREIS FAYETTE, TEXAS, IM SOMMER

Dieses Land felsenhart
durstig unter dem drahtigen Gras
den wilden Dornen
seine ausgetrockneten Teichaugen
starren in blaue Weite
heute morgen wochenlang
haben die Hoffnung auf Regen
aufgegeben wie wir unsre auf Tränen

dieses Land scheint sich dem
Warten der Dürre ergeben zu haben
ein Verzicht dem wir noch mit
unserer Arbeit trotzen

K 100

Today the heat fell
early in the morning from the
sky stretched without end to
the hazy horizon
it gets up again at noon
silently
explodes into the blue ocean
above roars
like ten desert lions
and one thirsty heart
a captive heart which
will dry up soon unprepared
to make concessions to be
reasonable

the evening too still full
of ambers
unthinkable that this
feverish intoxication
will ever pass
who would believe in such
fairy tales: country rain
and hoarfrost
reducing us again to our senses?

K 100

Heute fiel alle Hitze
schon früh aus dem Himmel
räkelte sich endlos bis
zum diesigen Horizont
stumm steht sie des Mittags
wieder auf
explodiert in den blauen
Ozean über sich
brüllt wie zehn Wüsten-
löwen
und ein durstiges
Herz
ein gefangenes
das bald verdorrt
nicht zu Zugeständnissen
bereit
nicht zu Vernunft

auch der Abend noch voller
Glut
es ist unvorstellbar
daß der Fieberrausch
sich einmal legen wird
wer mag solche Märchen
glauben daß Rieselregen
und Rauhreif uns auf unseren
Verstand reduzieren werden?

HEAT WAVE

From the cabin's cool air
I step into the hot light
a crystal clear sky above me
foot and head turn weightless
nowhere any animal in the
bone-dry landscape
spiders seem to hover exhausted
in shady corners instead of
spinning their nets
no bird-sounds no gliding of snakes
I step on the anthill
three emaciated fellows crawl out
tired and disappear again
right away it seems as if I am
alone in the world suddenly a
black moth falls straight out
of the oak leaves and in front of my foot
without fluttering a memory as from
obscure days a warning that
darkness will fall onto us
quite unexpectedly then the faint
chirping of one or two crickets
not a single leaf moves everything
still enjoys a brief span of time
until

HITZEWELLE

Aus der Hütte Kühle
geh ich in die heisse Helle
glasklar der Himmel über mir
Fuss und Haupt werden leicht
nirgends ein Tier in der
verdorrten Landschaft
Spinnen anstatt sich um ihr
Netz zu kümmern scheinen erschöpft
in schattigen Winkeln zu hocken
kein Vogellaut kein Schlangengehusch
ich stosse den Ameisenhügel an
da krabbeln entkräftet drei müde
Gesellen hervor und verschwinden
gleich wieder es ist als sei ich
allein auf der Welt plötzlich taumelt
ein schwarzer Falter aus dem Eichenlaub
senktecht ohne Flattern vor meinen
Fuss eine Erinnerung wie von dunklen
Tagen eine Warnung dass Finsteres
auf uns fallen wird ganz unverhofft
dann tönt das schwache Zirpen
einer oder zweier Grillen kein
Blatt regt sich noch ist allem
eine Spanne Zeit vergönnt bis

DROUGHT IN TEXAS

Only in these latitudes
and those even farther south
can heat claw into the soil
so that it cracks
cattle avoid the sun-exposed pasture
they hide in the woods as if afraid they might
be stolen at night
grass no longer grows
nor corn
nor soybeans
even for tarantulas and
scorpions it seems too hellishly hot
snakes peak only
at dawn and dusk
through the leaves of age-old tree-tops
but in front of my cabin
purple thistles bloom lavishly
and golden-yellow prickly pears
I ask you
when will you give in old man
to play high and mighty?
Get going! Leave the turf!
Let your younger brother —
in-season ascend to the throne
we are suffering we are waiting

DÜRRE IN TEXAS

Nur auf diesen und
noch südlicheren Breitengraden
kann sich Hitze so in den Boden
verkrallen dass er sich spaltet
Vieh meidet die sonnenpreisgegebene
Weide versteckt sich im
Gehölz als habe es Angst nachts
gestohlen zu werden
Gras wächst nicht
Mais nicht
Soja nicht
selbst für Taranteln und
Skorpione scheint es zu höllisch heiss
Schlangen lugen nur
in der Frühe und Dämmerung
aus dem Laub uralter Kronen
doch vor meiner Hütte
blühen üppig lila Disteln
goldgelbe Stachelbirnen-
Kakteen und ich frage:
wann gibts dus auf alter Mann
den Starken zu mimen?
Pack dich! Dank ab!
lass deinen jüngeren
Jahrzeitbruder die Thronfolge
antreten!
wir darben wir warten

ROUND TOP IN OCTOBER

When I plucked the sun
from the sky
I laughed because her
rays tickled my fingertips
the pastures chimed in and
so did the fish in the pond
the snow owl of whom I have
long been dreaming

Meadows I yelled
fish snow owl
listen tomorrow my
darling will come
so shouldn't I pluck
the sun the new moon the
stars from the sky?

Sure they nodded with
their leaves gull's wings
and I laughed
laughed loud
yes to be sure!

ROUND TOP IM OKTOBER

Als ich die Sonne
vom Himmel pflückte
lachte ich denn
ihre Strahlen krabbelten
mich an den Fingerkuppen
die Weiden lachten mit
die Fische im Weiher
die schneeige Eule von der
ich schon lange träume

Weiden rief ich .
Fische schneeige Eule
hört zui morgen kommt
mein Liebster zu mir
sollt ich da nicht Sonne
Neumond und Steerne vom
Himmel pflücken?

Gewiss doch nickten ihre
Halme Kiemen Schwingen
und ich lachte
lachte laut
ja gewiss doch!

HOARFROST

Slowly
tenderly
daintly ingenious crystals
dissolve
weak morning sun
warms
a stout hornet's
arthritic limbs
burrowed into a late dahlia
and a handful of
indolent ants
laboriously blazing their trail
rheumatic old men
painfully seeking
a small spot of sunlight
on the barn door
a hairy black sphere
rolls
at caterpillar speed
toward narrow fissure
to locate a warm winter dwelling
but the farmer draws a deep breath:
a good frost
cleanses the air

Translated by Minetta Altgelt Goyne

RAUHREIF

Langsam
zärtlich
lösen sich zierlich kunstvolle Kristalle
auf
schwache Vormittagssonne
wärmt
einer dicken Hummel
arthritische Glieder
in später Dahlie verkrochen
und eine handvoll
unemsiger Ameisen
die beschwerlich ihre Spur ziehn
rheumageplagte alte Männer
auf der Suche
nach einem sonnigen Fleckchen
an der Stalltür
rollt
behaarte schwarze Kugel
raupengeschwind
schmaler Spalte zu
warme Winterwohnung drin zu finden
der Bauer aber atmet auf:
ein guter Frost
reinigt die Luft

TEXAS AGAIN

When you were still unknown to me
I never felt
the desire
to experience you
feared
your notorious
climate and monotonous
landscape
also the cliché about
braggarts with big yaps
under big hats

accidentally cast
on your shore
shyly I tried to adapt
with elbows always poised ready to criticize
then what seemed impossible:
I discovered little affections
that grew
are growing still
perhaps I could
be firmly entwined
with you someday

one does not grow
accustomed
to everything but the friendly
life in your almost unbounded
spaces where water and air
are still unpolluted
an approach to happiness

translated by Minetta Altgelt Goyne

WIEDER TEXAS

Als du mir noch unbekannt
fühlte ich nie
den Wunsch
dich zu erfahren
fürchtete
dein berüchtigtes
Klima und die eintönige
Landschaft
auch das Klischee von den
Angebern mit großen Klappen
unter großen Hüten

durch Zufall an deine Küste
verschlagen
versuchte ich zages Anpassen
halbherzig
immer Kritik ellbogenbereit
dann was unmöglich schien:
ich entdeckte kleine
Zuneigungen
die wuchsen
wachsen noch
vielleicht könnte ich
eines Tages fest mit dir
verflochten sein

man gewöhnt sich
nicht
an alles aber das freundliche
Leben in deinen fast unbegrenzten
Weiten wo Wasser und Luft
noch unverseucht
eine Annäherung an das Glück

K 89

I live alone

Sometimes
Not too often
I open
My wound
A mere crack
Soundlessly let in
The pain
Sharply
Or dully

Then I know
That I am not yet dead

K 89

Ich lebe allein

Manchmal
Nicht zu oft
Offne ich
Um cinen Spalt
Meine Wunde
Lasse lautlos
Den Schmerz ein
Scharf
Auch dumpf

Dann merke ich
Daß ich noch nicht gestorben bin

NEW YEAR

Always the co-existence of opposites:
The fluttering of roused scared
wild-doves — silent hibernating of
snakes
the cracking in forest and brush
by deer and cattle
a jet draws with a white crayon
on the pastel blue New Year's sky
the trace of our flights:
intended and remembered

NEUJAHR

Immer die Gleichzeitigkeit der Gegensätze:
Geflatter ängstliches aufgescheuchter
Wildtauben — stummer Winterschlaf der
Schlangen
Knacken im Gehölz unter Fuss von Reh
und Rind
am blassblauen Neujahrshimmel
eines Düsenfliegers mit weissem Stift
gezeichnete Spur unsrer Flüge:
geplanter — erinnerter

K 103

When you come from the city
it takes a while till
your ear learns again
to hear silence
>   far away fluttering of fearful pigeons
>   rustling of oak leaves
>   cedars
>   lisping of hip-high grass
>   armadillos pawing the ground
>   a nut falling
>   silent soliloquy

at long last when you
understand the language of
solitude once more you must hurry
back to the landscape of

>   motors roaring
>   blowing of horns
>   thundering jets
>   into the tower of Babel

K 103

Kommst du aus der Stadt
dauert es seine Weile
bis dein Ohr wieder lernt
die Stille zu hören

> fernes Aufflattern ängstlicher Tauben
> Blätterraunen von Eichen
> Zedern
> Lispeln hüfthoher Halme
> Scharren des Gürteltiers
> Fallen der Nuss
> lautloses Selbstgespräch

endlich
wenn es die Sprache der
Einsamkeit wieder versteht
musst du zurück in die
Landschaft des

> Motorgedröhnes
> der Hupen und
> donnernden Düsenflieger
> in den Turm von Babel

LOG CABIN

Behind dewberry bushes and purple thistles
the self-made split-rail cedar fence drenched
with sweat (damn why is the wood so hard?!)
you toiled to drag the smooth
stoneplates here which now invite your foot: feel

how cool we are
they lead to the grass-framed porch
where blind window-eyes stare at you
why do you intrude into our loneliness?
Inquire the shrieking hinges and
bed and chair and table and
the old Franklin-stove they all
silently lament: who has rendered us so useless?
No longer needed we mildew in the humid heat
and
yet once we were useful
well-made and appreciated
cared for by a woman's hands
knocked smeared drummed upon
by children's fingers where have they gone?

You push the shutters open
gaze at the pinkish white of the wild
cherry in front of you
and laugh: don't worry
I'll stay with you
till it is time to part

LOG CABIN

Hinter Brombeerhecke und lila Disteln
der schweissbetropfte Zaun aus
selbstgespaltener Zeder (verdammt warum ist dein Holz
                        so hart?!)
so glatt die mühsam angeschleppten
Platten laden den Fuss ein: fühl
unsre Kühle
führen dich auf gräserumrahmte Veranda
wo blinde Fensteraugen auf dich
starren
was dringst du in unsre Einsamkeit?
fragt kreischend die Türangel und
Bett und Stuhl und Tisch
der alte Franklin-Herd sie klagen
stumm: wer hat so nutzlos uns gemacht?
aufs Altengleise abgestellt? Ungebraucht
verschimmeln wir in feuchter Hitze und
waren doch einst brauchbar
wohlgestaltet und geschätzt
von einer Frauenhand umsorgt
von Kinderhand beklopft beschmiert
betrommelt wo sind die Hände hin?

Du stösst die Laden auf:
Schaust das Rosaweiss der wilden
Kirsche vor euren Nasen und
du lachst: habt keine Angst
ich bleibe bei euch
bis zum Abschied

OLD CEMETERY IN TEXAS

The constant hitting of pebbles
against the metal when
you travel on the gravel road
even at ten miles per hour
peng peng
ping ping

hardly a tree
to cast some shade
on the grave markers
many in German: "unsere gute Mutter
                    mein lieber Mann
                    unser Engelchen"

born in Oldenburg
in Detmold the immigrants
were young stranded in the
glimmering heat of this region

grand- and great-grand-children
monolingual by now lay plastic
wreaths on the graves of the
unknown it is
fashionable to remember one's forbears
and were the language not as hard
the tongues not as heavy
perhaps it might become popular
to learn German again

an idle hope of
aging teachers

meanwhile waiting behind the
lone cedar at the gate stands
death

ALTER FRIEDHOF IN TEXAS

Auf den Schotterstraßen
andauernder Steinschlag gegen
das Blech selbst bei zehn Meilen
pro Stunde
peng peng
ping ping

Kaum ein Baum
spendet den Steinen
Schatten
viele in deutscher Sprache: "unsere gute Mutter
                        mein lieber Mann
                        unser Engelchen"

noch in Oldenburg geboren
in Detmold jung verschlug es
in die flirrende Hitze dieses
Landstrichs die Auswanderer

Enkel und Urenkel
nur einsprachig noch legen
Plastikkränze auf die Gräber
der Ungekannten
es ist Mode sich der Vorfahren
zu erinnern und wären Sprache
und Zungen nicht so schwer
vielleicht würde es Mode
wieder deutsch zu lernen

eine vergebliche Hoffnung
alternder Lehrer

inzwischen wartet schon hinter der
einsamen Zeder am Tor
der Tod

This is a love story:
He said I want you green Lorca-green
another one painted light and scenery
green but the third one sent me
green words green pictures trees
large and small all kinds of moss
ferns grasses hills and valleys a green
brook and even the trace of sky
over a clearing lindengreen
a green heart that was the essence of his being

Dies ist die Geschichte einer Liebe:
Er sagte ich wünsche dich grün Lorca-grün
ein anderer malte Licht und Landschaft
grün aber der dritte schenkte mir
grüne Worte grüne Bilder Bäume grosse
und kleine aller Arten Moose Farne
Gräser Hügel und Täler einen grünen
Bach und selbst die Andeutung des
Himmels über einer Lichtung lindgrün
ein grünes Herz so war sein Wesen